CLASSIC
StoryTellers

BEVERLY CLEARY

Mitchell Lane
PUBLISHERS

P.O. Box 196
Hockessin, Delaware 19707

Titles in the Series

C L A S S I C
StoryTellers

BEVERLY CLEARY

Michèle Griskey

StoryTellers StoryTellers StoryTellers Story Tellers StoryTellers StoryTellers Story Tellers Story

Printing   1   2   3   4   5   6   7   8

Library of Congress Cataloging-in-Publication Data
Griskey, Michèle.
      Beverly Cleary/by Michèle Griskey.
            p. cm.—(Classic storytellers)
      Includes bibliographical references and index.
      ISBN 1-58415-457-8 (library bound: alk. paper)
1. Cleary, Beverly—Juvenile literature. 2. Authors, American—20th century—Biography—Juvenile literature. I. Title. II. Series.
PS3553.L3914Z5925 2006
813'.6—dc22
                                                                    2005036697
ISBN-10: 1-58415-457-8   ISBN-13: 978-158415-457-0

ABOUT THE AUTHOR: Michèle Griskey has a BA in writing and an MA in English, with concentrations in literature and creative writing. She teaches writing, research, and philosophy for the University of Phoenix Online. She has written several biographies for Mitchell Lane Publishers, including *Harriet Beecher Stowe* and *Ray Bradbury*. She first read *Ramona The Pest* when she was in the fourth grade and has been a fan of Cleary's work ever since. Michèle also writes fiction for middle grade and teen readers and lives on an island in Washington's Puget Sound with her family.

PHOTO CREDITS: Cover, pp. 1, 3, 6, 11 Getty Images; p. 16 Jamie Kondrchek; p. 20 Library of Congress; pp. 23, 28, 36 Getty Images

PUBLISHER'S NOTE: This story is based on the author's extensive research, which she believes to be accurate. Documentation of such research is contained on page 46.
        The internet sites referenced herein were active as of the publication date. Due to the fleeting nature of some web sites, we cannot guarantee they will all be active when you are reading this book.

                                                                                    PLB

Contents

BEVERLY CLEARY

Michèle Griskey

*For Your Information

Beverly Cleary draws inspiration from her own childhood to make her characters interesting and believable. This is what has made her work timeless and well loved by several generations of children.

Chapter 1

BLACKBIRDS AND BLUEBIRDS

The magic of reading . . . For as long as she could remember, Beverly Bunn had been under the spell of books. More than anything, she wanted to learn how to read. She thought about all the books in the library her mother had taken her to see. But her journey began with a struggle she hadn't anticipated.

After she became ill with smallpox and missed weeks of school, Beverly reluctantly returned to the first grade. She didn't like her teacher, Miss Falb. She didn't like her even more after she put Beverly in the dreaded "Blackbird" reading group. Beverly loved stories. She loved the fairy and folk tales her mother read to her. Before she started the first grade, Beverly's mother read the play *The Blue Bird,* about two children and their quest for happiness; Beverly had been sure that she would find happiness when she started school and learned how to read. But school wasn't what she had expected. In addition to dealing with a teacher who didn't seem to like children very much, Beverly found her first-grade reading book dull. She also found the use of certain letters in words baffling. "What was that *h* doing in John?"[1] she wondered.

Because she'd been home for so long, Beverly had fallen behind. She described how the school was organized: "The class had been divided into three groups: Bluebirds, who found happiness in the seats by the window; Redbirds, who sat in the middle seats; and Blackbirds, who sat by the blackboard, far from the sunlight."[2] Beverly sat in the back with the other Blackbirds and felt fear every time she was called up to read flash cards. A series of unfamiliar words rushed past her eyes. She knew only a few of them, and the rest remained a mystery. It was frustrating and humiliating. How could a girl who liked stories so much be put in the lowest reading group? She just wanted something interesting to read.

All of Beverly's hopes for school and reading vanished. She began to plead with her mother to stay home. Despite her begging, Beverly had to continue. Her mother reminded her of her pioneer ancestors and that, like them, she should stick it out. Beverly remembered, "I was fed up with all of those pioneer ancestors, who only faced danger and starvation and did not have Miss Falb for a teacher."[3]

If Beverly could have looked into the future, she would have found that the following year would bring a much nicer teacher, Miss Marius, who would teach her how to read, and a much more interesting book to use. Then the year after that, Beverly would find that reading on her own was a wonderful experience. If Beverly could have looked far into the future, she would have found that she would grow up to become a popular and award-winning author who created stories for children like herself who just wanted something interesting and fun to read. She would find the bluebird of happiness in her writing.

FYInfo

The Blue Bird
by Maurice Maeterlinck

Maurice Maeterlinck, a Belgian writer, was born in 1862. Influenced by the French literary movement called symbolism, Maeterlinck began writing poetry. He sought to use symbols to represent ideas in his writing. He went on to write more poetry, and then turned his attention to playwriting.

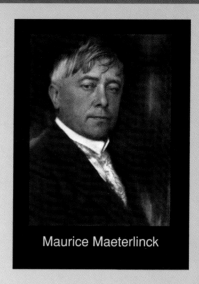

Maurice Maeterlinck

The symbolic blue bird represented happiness in his play *The Blue Bird.* This very popular children's play was performed often during the early part of the twentieth century. It tells the story of two children, Mytyl and her brother, Tyltyl, who fall asleep and meet the good fairy Bérylune. The fairy helps them in their search to find happiness in the shape of a blue bird. They journey with their pet dog and cat to a fantasy world full of dangers and mystery, including the land of memory, the palace of happiness, and the kingdom of the future. When they awaken, they realize the blue bird was in their own house all along. A neighbor asks the children if she can have the bird for her dying child. The bird heals the child, but then it flies away. At the end, Mytyl and Tyltyl ask the audience to return the bird if they find it. The play shows how we need not look far to find happiness in our lives.

This play was later created as films in different time periods. Two silent films were made (in 1910 and 1918), and then a film with sound was made in the 1940s featuring popular child star Shirley Temple. In the 1970s, Russians and Americans filmed a version as a joint effort.

Maurice Maeterlinck wrote other plays and books of essays over the years. He won the Nobel Prize in Literature in 1911. He fled Europe during World War II and lived in the United States before returning France. He died in 1949.

The long and potentially dangerous journey on the Oregon Trail linked the eastern part of the United States to the western territories. The challenges didn't stop thousands of people from making the journey to Oregon and California. Many, like these pioneers, traveled by covered wagon and camped along the way.

Chapter 2

COUNTRY GIRL, CITY GIRL

Beverly Atlee Bunn was born on April 12, 1916, in McMinnville, Oregon. Her mother, Mable Atlee, came from Michigan and moved to the West to teach school. Mable met a young man named Chester Lloyd Bunn at a store that Mable's parents owned in Banks, Oregon. After they married on December 26, 1907, Mable and Chester bought a farm in Yamhill, Oregon. This is where Beverly lived for the first six years of her life.

In the 1800s, Beverly's father's ancestors had traveled across the Oregon Trail until they reached Oregon. These ancestors endured a long journey and hardships, of which Beverly's parents constantly reminded their young daughter. Over and over again, Beverly heard, "Remember your pioneer ancestors,"[1] until she began to dislike these people whom she was supposed to copy.

Beverly recalls her early days on the farm as a time when she was left to find her own adventures. She remembered growing up: "I had freedom for self-amusement, for looking, smelling, examining, exploring. No one cared if I got dirty. My parents were much too hard-working to be concerned about a little dirt."[2]

Beverly enjoyed her life in Yamhill. She spent time gathering wildflowers, meeting her neighbors, and going to town. Many of her relatives still lived in and around Yamhill, and Beverly felt very welcomed and cared for there.

Beverly's mother taught her a great deal about how to behave, and she also read to and shared her interests with her daughter. Once, Mrs. Bunn decided to begin a library, which required raising money to purchase books. According to Beverly, the library was "a china cabinet in a smoky-smelling room over a bank."[3] Despite its simplicity, the little library opened up a world of possibility for young Beverly. Her mother's passion for books was one of the earliest influences on the love of literature Beverly would develop. Beverly remembers treasuring the two books that she owned, *Mother Goose* and *The Story of the Three Bears*. She begged her mother to read new books of fairy tales and adventures from the library.

The idyllic life out in the country didn't last, however. Though Chester Bunn had a successful farm, he couldn't get the prices he needed for his harvest. The economic struggles of the 1920s had hit home. Many farmers were not getting as much money as they once did for their crops. Eventually the financial strain became too much. The Bunn family decided to rent their farm and move to Portland, Oregon.

In Portland, everything was different. Instead of wide-open farmland for amusement, six-year-old Beverly found noisy city streets with lots of neighborhood children to play with. They roller-skated and made stilts out of coffee cans and twine. These stilts would later be featured in Beverly's book *Ramona and Her Father.*

Mr. Bunn preferred farmwork over his new job as a night guard at a bank, but Mrs. Bunn was happy to be away from the duties of a farmer's wife. Beverly made her first trip to the Portland library with her mother. She was amazed at the amount of books she saw in the children's section. Years later she remembered how it impressed her: " 'All for children?' I asked. 'All for children,' said Mother. That room seemed so magic that I wanted to be part of all it offered. The course of my life was set."[4]

Beverly began first grade determined to love school and learn how to read as quickly as possible, but Miss Falb didn't inspire her to learn. The humiliation of being placed in the Blackbird reading group didn't help. Beverly also heard her parents talking about a huge earthquake that rattled Japan. The 1923 earthquake and the fire that followed killed tens of thousands of people in the cities of Tokyo and Yokohama. Beverly internalized this tragic event and began to develop irrational fears. She began to fear that she would die at night while her father was at work. The combination of her fears of school and dying didn't make the first grade a good experience for Beverly.

Fortunately, the following year went better. Miss Marius, who was kind and patient, taught Beverly how to read. Beverly soon found she enjoyed reading, but she decided for some reason that she would never read outside of school. This seemed strange to her mother, who considered reading a pleasure and wanted Beverly to enjoy reading anywhere.

The following year brought some improvements for the Bunn family. Beverly's father found a new job where he could work days instead of nights in a bank lobby. He wore a revolver under his suit to protect the bank in case someone tried to rob it. The Bunn family also moved to a different house and enrolled Beverly in a new school.

Chapter 2   COUNTRY GIRL, CITY GIRL

In third grade Beverly made another breakthrough in reading. In a small library at her church, she found *The Dutch Twins,* the first book that she would read outside of school. She remembered, "Suddenly I was reading and enjoying what I read! It was a miracle. I was happy in a way I had not been happy since starting school."[5] Many years later, Beverly would encourage adults to model reading as a pastime, noting, "Children should learn that reading is pleasure, not just something that teachers make you do in school."[6]

Their new house was close to the Columbia River Gorge, so winter brought icy storms that were hard to endure. Despite the challenging weather, Beverly found new adventures. She experienced her first publishing success when she wrote book reviews for the *Oregon Journal.* She also began seeing silent movies, like the exciting pirate adventures of *The Sea Hawk* and *Peter Pan.*

The end of the school year brought another move to another house, which was near the school Beverly had attended in the first and second grades. There, Beverly was back around the children and events of downtown Portland. She had her first big lessons about writing when a store announced an essay contest sponsored by Ked Shoes. Many students at school talked about what they were going to write for the contest. The essay was supposed to be about an animal, and Beverly wrote hers on the beaver. She won the contest and the prize—two dollars. The storeowner told her that no one else had entered the contest. Beverly said, "This incident was one of the most valuable lessons in writing I ever learned. Try! Others will talk about writing but may never get around to trying."[7]

Beverly continued through grade school and settled into her life in Portland, but her parents were unhappy. Raised on a farm doing work outside, Chester Bunn was miserable working in a bank all day. He wanted to go back to the family farm. Mrs. Bunn disagreed. She didn't like the life of a farmer's wife, with its countless chores. She liked living in the city. Sometimes Beverly heard them arguing at night. Mr. Bunn, who had been quiet, became moody and got angry easily. He was frustrated and felt trapped.[8]

Music entered Beverly's life, but she didn't enjoy it. First she was required to sing alone in Miss Johnson's singing class. The thought of singing solo terrified her. When she was in the school Christmas operetta, *The Cruise of the Trundle Bed,* she refused to sing in that as well. At her mother's request, Beverly began taking piano lessons, but she found it tiresome—especially when the child across the street could play better than she.

Meanwhile, Beverly read many fairy tales. She discovered the Greek legend of Persephone and her mother, Demeter. In the story, Persephone is captured and taken to the underworld, and Demeter searches for her daughter. Her sorrow causes the world to become cold and barren. Finally she finds her, and she makes an agreement with Persephone's husband, the ruler of the underworld. Persephone is allowed to return to the surface every year for six months, but then she must spend the other six months in the underworld. When Persephone returns to the surface, Demeter is happy, and the world flourishes again. When Persephone goes back to her husband, Demeter's sadness again makes the earth barren. The myth explained to the ancient Greeks why there were seasons. Beverly felt that the story reflected her own life. "I read that beautiful myth over and over and each time felt solace," she remembered. "I also came to understand that we cannot expect flowers to bloom continuously in life."[9]

After repeated bouts with tonsillitis, Beverly had to have an operation to remove her tonsils. The children talked about it at school, and one boy teased her about it. She was scared when she went to the hospital, but after a quick recovery and lots of ice cream, she felt better and stayed healthy.

The years passed and Beverly's parents finally decided to sell the farm in Yamhill. With the money, they were able to buy a house in Portland, and Beverly was sent to an orthodontist to get braces for her teeth. They also bought a car and took Sunday drives to places outside of Portland and in Willamette Valley, up to Mount Hood,

Mount Hood, at 11,237 feet, is the highest mountain in Oregon. Located near Portland, it has long been a popular tourist site. When Beverly's parents bought a car, the family would drive out to Mount Hood for the day.

and along the Columbia River. Beverly visited many places her pioneer ancestors had lived.

Beverly began the seventh grade under a new school design called the platoon system, which was similar to middle schools or junior high schools in present times. Students learned traditional subjects like math and grammar, but they were also sent to other rooms in "platoons" for extra subjects like art, science, and physical education. In a course on nature, the teacher, Miss Crawford, did something unusual. She told everyone the story of Victor Hugo's classic novel *Les Miserables.* Though it didn't relate to the topic of nature, Beverly and the other students looked forward to hearing about the adventures of the character Jean Valjean. Her experience with Miss Crawford taught her the value of a good story that captures the attention of the audience.

Beverly also had a new reading teacher, who was the school librarian. One day in class, Miss Smith asked the students to pretend they were living in George Washington's time and to write a letter to someone discussing an experience. When students complained, Miss Smith explained that they should use their imaginations. "I was excited," Beverly recalled. "All my life, Mother had told me to use my imagination, but I had never expected to be asked, or even allowed, to use it in school."[10]

Beverly wrote from the point of view of a character who had to kill a pet chicken to help feed George Washington and his troops at Valley Forge. Miss Smith read Beverly's letter to the class and praised her for her original work.

In another assignment, Miss Smith asked the students to write an essay about a favorite book character. Unable to make up her mind which character to choose, Beverly wrote about a girl who traveled through "Bookland" to talk to different literary characters. Just as she had discovered the joys of reading years earlier, Beverly now discovered the joy of writing. She remembered how that assignment affected her: "As rain beat against the windows, a feeling of peace came over me as I wrote far beyond the required length of the essay. I had discovered the pleasure of writing, and to this day, whenever it rains, I feel the urge to write."[11]

Miss Smith again singled out Beverly's work and read it to the class. Then she said something that would determine Beverly's future. She said, "When Beverly grows up, she should write children's books."[12] That is exactly what Beverly would do.

Beverly told her family what she wanted to do, and her mother suggested that she have another job as well that would supply a steady income. Since Beverly enjoyed the library so much, she decided that she would be a librarian as well.

Not all of Beverly's school writing experiences were positive. In one class in the eighth grade, her teacher, Mrs. Drake, asked the students to write a descriptive paragraph. Beverly decided to write about an incident that had happened when she was on vacation with her parents. A mule deer had stepped out in front of the car just as the sun was rising. Fortunately, the car was stopped in time, but the image stuck in her mind. Beverly turned in the assignment with confidence, but was dismayed when it was returned. Mrs. Drake had covered Beverly's paragraph with corrections. This influenced Beverly's writing, for she is known for her simple, easy-to-read style. She explained, "For years I avoided writing description, and children told me they liked my books 'because there isn't any description in them.' "[13]

FYInfo

The Oregon Trail

The Oregon Trail was the overland route to the West during the 1800s. Finding the Oregon Trail took some time.

U.S. President Thomas Jefferson knew that Alexander Mackenzie, a British subject, had gone overland from the East to the Pacific. Mackenzie reached the ocean in 1793. In 1803, Jefferson sent Meriwether Lewis and William Clark on an expedition to find their own passage to the west coast. The journey was kept secret because at that time, the United States didn't extend all the way to the Pacific, and Lewis and Clark would be crossing British territory. After a long, difficult journey, and with help from many Native Americans, Lewis and Clark reached the Pacific Ocean in 1805.

Though Lewis and Clark had crossed the continent, their route was not the easiest way. To cross the Rockies, they had used the difficult Lolo Pass. A few years later another explorer, Robert Stuart, stumbled upon South Pass, a twenty-mile-wide gap in the Rockies. It was wide enought for wagon trains to pass through easily.

The Oregon Trail starts in Independence, Missouri, and ends in Oregon City, Oregon. It follows the Platte River, goes through the mountains, follows the Snake River, and ends up at the Columbia River. Of course, people started from places all over, and some ended up in places besides Oregon City. Many traveled south to California instead.

The great migration didn't happen right away. Some reports from explorers made the journey seem less than worthwhile. Zebulon Pike and later Steven Long gave unpleasant descriptions of what are now parts of the Midwest. Pike called it a Great American Desert, and farmers didn't want to travel to a wasteland. Long confirmed Pike's description. With these negative reports of the West, the popularity of westward expansion didn't really catch on until the mid-1800s. Yet more and more people did go west, and they found ideal places to start farms and build cities. The gold rush that began in 1849 brought more people over the trail.

By the 1890s, the West was no longer a mystery. Estimates show that 80,000 to perhaps 200,000 people traveled along the Oregon Trail.

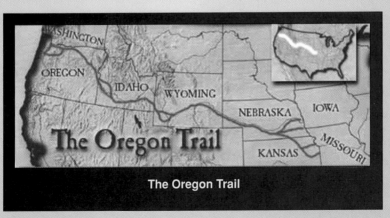

The Oregon Trail

A little girl in a ragged dress peers out of a rundown house during the Great Depression. The Great Depression had a huge impact on the lives of many people living in the United States during the 1930s. The failure of crops and the lack of employment forced people to live as simply as possible. Survival became their primary goal.

Chapter 3

WRITING AND BOYS

The Great Depression was sweeping the nation. The stock market crashed, banks closed, and many people lost their jobs. In 1930, in the summer before Beverly began high school, the Depression hit home. Mr. Bunn lost his job at the bank. During that summer, everyone in the family worked diligently to save money. Mrs. Bunn made simple meals, they all brushed their teeth with baking soda, and Mr. Bunn sharpened his razor on the inside of a glass to make it last. Mr. Bunn went out regularly, anxiously looking for a new job. Life in their house grew very tense until he found a job again, which happened later in the fall.

Years later, Beverly would use the hardships that her family faced in a story about a girl named Ramona Quimby. Like Beverly's real-world experience, in *Ramona and Her Father,* Ramona's father loses his job and the family must make adjustments to get by.

Beverly began high school with her good friend Claudine. She earned an E+ (Excellent-plus) on a story called "Diary of a Tree-Sitter," in which she followed her mother's advice of writing simply and with humor. A second story, "The Green Christmas," found its way into the school paper. A revised version of this story later became a chapter in Beverly's first book, *Henry Huggins,* when green paint spills all over Henry's face and hair, and he is relieved from playing the most dreaded role in the Christmas play.

During this time Beverly learned a great deal of poetry in school. She discovered poets of her time, such as Carl Sandburg. Beverly and Claudine also read on their own. They particularly enjoyed Westerns and read the works of B. M. Bower and Zane Grey. They also listened to the radio, went to movies (which were no longer silent), and made fun of the examples in their grammar book.

At home Beverly had a tense relationship with her mother. From early on, Mrs. Bunn was prone to giving her only daughter advice and criticism. As Beverly grew older, the tension increased. Once, after making a dress for Beverly, her mother decided that the bow on the jacket should be cut off. Beverly protested because she liked the bow. One day, when she came home from school, she found her mother had cut off the bow. Another time a pen pal had sent Beverly an animal skin from Africa. Her mother wanted Beverly to throw it out, but Beverly liked it. When she discovered it missing, she found out her mother had tossed it in the garbage. The older Beverly got, the more she felt as if her mother meddled needlessly in her life. This became particularly troublesome when Beverly began dating boys.

Once when Beverly went with Claudine and Claudine's mother to the Masonic Lodge to deliver Christmas decorations, the two friends went upstairs to watch a dance taking place. This was the era when dancers dressed up—men in suits and women in formal gowns. Claudine and Beverly sat on the side to watch the older, beautifully dressed dancers when a man wearing a tuxedo asked Beverly to dance.

A young woman and her daughter enjoy time together in front of a radio. In the 1920s and 1930s, many families sat around the radio listening to dramatic shows, news, and music. In those days, radios could be as large as some modern television sets.

Beverly felt very self-conscious in her school clothes attempting to dance with an elegantly dressed man in his twenties. After this experience she began taking ballroom dancing lessons. One day a new student arrived who was older than the high school guys. He gave Beverly and her mother a ride home after class. This man, whom Beverly calls Gerhart in her memoir, started spending more and more time with Beverly. Though she felt that she had little in common with Gerhart, she continued to see him. In part, Mrs. Bunn encouraged the relationship. Gerhart also offered Beverly a break from her home and her mother, but she felt disappointed because she expected to be happier. She had been led to believe that she was supposed to go out with a boy, fall in love, and live happily ever after. She didn't feel happy with Gerhart and became increasingly confused.

English classes continued to give Beverly opportunities to write. In one class, she was asked to write an outline before she put together a story. She found this very difficult. Creating an outline first seemed to stifle her creativity. She took a journalism course that helped her develop her skills as a writer. "Even though I still had trouble with outlines," she admitted, "journalism taught me to set words on paper faster and with better organization than I had been able to do before."[1] Meanwhile, she was asked to write a script for the Girls' League Show, which would raise money for a scholarship. She wrote the script with another student. It was a romantic drama, and the teacher in charge of producing the play wanted Beverly to play the lead. She assured the girl that she was just as pretty as the other popular girls in school. Thrilled at being called pretty, Beverly agreed to take the role. She said, "No one had ever called me pretty before. I suddenly felt pretty. Pretty me! Pretty me!"[2] Mrs. Bunn was equally excited that her daughter had been given the lead role.

Going to school in the 1930s had some of the same challenges that students face today. Students formed groups based on who was the most popular. Right after Beverly got the lead role in the play, a popular girl from the Girl's League called and asked her to withdraw from the part. She pointed out that Beverly didn't have any of the nice clothes that would be needed for the role of a rich young woman. Though Beverly was dismayed that the other more popular girls didn't want her in the play, she followed her mother's advice and stood up to the challenge. Beverly refused to back down and kept the role. Others, when they heard what happened, pitched in and provided Beverly with some elegant clothes to use for the part.

Gerhart continued to see Beverly. She wondered why a boy who was older and had nothing in common with her liked her so much. Among other things, Gerhart made fun of her love of literature and writing. She was totally stunned when one night during the summer between her junior and senior years of high school, Gerhart asked her to marry him. She remembers her reaction: "*Marry* him? Marriage to anyone, especially Gerhart, was of no interest to me when my life had not really begun."[3] Beverly refused his offer, but he continued to see her, which she didn't understand. Beverly began to feel trapped.

When she started her senior year of high school, her future looked bleak. Her father was unhappy with his job, and both her parents worried about having enough money for retirement. They also worried about Beverly's future. At this time there were few jobs available for young respectable women, and college was very expensive. Though Beverly's grades were good, she was unsure if she could get a scholarship for college. The other option was marriage, but Beverly knew she wasn't ready for that. What was she going to do?

One day a letter came that gave her a great deal to think about. It was from her great-aunt Elizabeth's daughter, Verna. She invited Beverly to come down to California and live at her house so that

Beverly could attend the junior college in Ontario (California junior colleges didn't charge tuition). Mrs. Bunn immediately dismissed the idea as impractical, but Mr. Bunn decided that Beverly should go. Beverly was thrilled. She needed a change in her life.

In a dramatics class, Beverly read the poem "Patterns" by Amy Lowell for a presentation. She felt the poem reflected her own life, she wrote, "because I too, had been 'held rigid to a pattern,' and quite long enough."[4] When she performed, she confessed, she "finished with tears in my eyes and a break in my voice. I had enough pent-up anguish to carry me through any number of renditions of 'Patterns.' "[5]

Beverly graduated from Grant High School in 1934. That summer she had her braces taken off and prepared herself to go to California. The day finally arrived when she could escape the critical eye of her mother and unwanted advances from Gerhart.

FYInfo

The Great Depression

A 1930s soup kitchen

In the 1930s, the United States endured an economic crisis. Many factors from the previous decade combined to cause the hardships. One factor was that crop prices for farmers began to drop. Farmers couldn't make the money they once could for their harvests. Factories churned out large amounts of products, but there were more products than people needed. Investing in the stock market had become very popular. A lot of people borrowed money to invest, which wasn't a good idea. So many people invested that the value of stocks in the stock market dropped. People panicked. They pulled their money out, causing the stock market to crash in 1929. They tried to get their money out of bank accounts. Many of the banks didn't have enough money to give all the people. Banks failed and people lost their savings. Then people lost their jobs. In addition, in the 1930s, an eight-year-long drought in the South and Midwest caused the Dust Bowl, enormous dust storms churned up from the dry, overworked farmland. Many farmers lost their crops and their money.

People had to make drastic changes in their lives. Many of the farmers migrated to other places, leaving their homes to find work in the city or in other farming areas that hadn't been affected by the drought. Many people didn't have enough money to even eat, and charity soup kitchens were set up in cities. People waited in long lines to get a simple meal.

The economic crisis also spread to other parts of the world, including Europe. It took a very long time for the United States to see prosperous times again. It wasn't until 1939, while Franklin Delano Roosevelt was the U.S. president, that the economy started to recover. Among other strategies, Roosevelt created domestic programs to get people back to work and to help them in tough times. For example, the Works Progress Administration found work for 8.5 million people, and the Social Security Program was established to help people in need, especially those over the age of sixty-five.

Beverly (right) didn't know that when she moved to California in 1936, she would meet the love of her life. Clarence Cleary (left), the man whom Beverly would marry, always supported Beverly's desire to write. The Clearys now live in Carmel, California.

Chapter 4

ESCAPE TO CALIFORNIA

Beverly felt a mix of joy and fear: joy because she was going on an adventure and was about to face a new life; fear because she knew her parents expected a great deal from her education. Her parents, she felt, had suffered during the Depression. Her mother had a lot of energy, but she overwhelmed Beverly by trying to control her daughter's life. While Beverly's father had endured working in a bank vault in the city, he had missed the farming life. "Now I was the focus of my parents' hopes; I must be educated no matter what sacrifices had to be made," she wrote years later. "I longed to have my parents happy, to share, not sacrifice. The burden of guilt was heavy."[1]

After a tiring bus ride to San Francisco, where Beverly stayed with some former neighbors from Portland, and another night in Los Angeles, Beverly arrived in Ontario, California. She stayed with Verna, who worked as a librarian; Verna's husband, Fred, who taught physical education at the high school; and their two children, Virginia and Atlee. Fred's mother, Mother Clapp, also lived with them. Beverly was amazed at the warm weather, the orange grove in the yard, and the avocado tree outside her bedroom window. It was so different from green, rainy Portland.

Beverly found taking classes at Chaffey Junior College enjoyable and the people friendly. As with high school, she sought to do well in her college courses. She met a young man named Paul, whom she found a lot nicer to be with than Gerhart had been. Living in Ontario was more relaxing than living at home. She wrote letters to Claudine to tell her how happy she was.

That winter, Beverly experienced her first earthquake. She watched the drama of the men who had to burn smudge pots to keep the orange trees from freezing on the few nights of the year that the temperatures dropped. She also found fun things to do, like going to dances with Paul and going for drives in the desert.

Unfortunately, the school year ended with conflict. Great-Aunt Elizabeth (Verna's mother) came to visit and began to criticize Beverly. She told Beverly that she hadn't been helping out enough around the house, and she disapproved of how Beverly looked in her tight dresses. Several months of eating avocados had caused Beverly to put on weight for the first time in her life, and she didn't have money to buy better fitting clothes. Verna told Beverly that she wouldn't be able to stay at the house the next year, because both Elizabeth and Mother Clapp would be staying with them. When Beverly got on the Greyhound bus to return to Portland, she was crying. How would she make it back to school in September?

All summer Beverly worried about what to do. She remembered hearing about a girl named Norma from Washington State who would also need a new place to stay at college. Desperate for a solution, Beverly contacted Norma. They worked out a plan to share an apartment in Ontario and attend Chaffey again.

Beverly loved her new independence, living in a little apartment. She and Norma, a physical education major, got along well. Beverly also found opportunities to make money. She did some knitting and worked as a substitute librarian. At school, Beverly's English teacher, Mr. Palmer, assigned his class a daily 300-word paper until someone earned an A. Beverly wrote and wrote. She began to grow desperate for more essay ideas. Finally, after she wrote an essay based on her memory of a man selling violets in a restaurant (an incident from the Depression, when many people were forced to sell things for a living), Beverly earned the first A for the class. Again she was reminded of the value of writing from her own experience. Later, when she was required to write a short story, she had trouble coming up with a plot. She wrote about her own experiences as a child struggling to read in school. She remembered, "Mr. Palmer gave me an unqualified A, reading my story to the class, and said, 'This story is nothing to be ashamed of,' lighting me with joy with this, for him, lavish praise. Without knowing it, I had begun to write the story of my life."[2]

The following year Beverly began attending the University of California at Berkeley, or Cal, as it was called then. She hoped that she would eventually be accepted to their graduate librarian program. She stayed at Stebbins Hall, a cooperative house for female students. Beverly found the demands of the university more challenging than the junior college, but she was determined to study hard.

Every other week, an Assembly Dance was held in the school gym. At one of these gatherings, a tall, dark-haired, blue-eyed man asked Beverly to dance; his name was Clarence Cleary. Beverly and Clarence began spending more and more time together. He was six years older than she. When her mother found out that Beverly, who was raised as a Protestant, was seeing a Catholic man, she told Beverly she shouldn't date Clarence. Beverly ignored her mother.

Chapter 4   ESCAPE TO CALIFORNIA

During her second (and final) year at Cal, Beverly continued to see Clarence, who proposed to her. She agreed but told him she wanted to finish college, go to library school, and work one year before they tied the knot. She received an acceptance letter from the University of Washington to attend the School of Librarianship. It looked as if the future was full of promise.

Unfortunately, not everyone was pleased with Beverly's prospects. Mrs. Bunn wrote her daughter that she shouldn't marry Clarence and wouldn't get approval from her parents. In addition to her personal problems, Beverly was required to take an English comprehensive exam to graduate. The first part of the exam was very difficult, but she managed to do better on the second part. Overall she got a passing grade and could continue with her education.

In the fall, Beverly moved to Seattle to learn how to be a librarian. She liked going to library school. In the spring she lived at her parents' house in Portland and did practical work at various libraries in the city. She went back to Seattle and graduated. Beverly was told of an opening in Los Angeles, but her mother said that she didn't have the money to send her to California. Beverly wondered whether her mother was trying to keep her away from Clarence, who now lived in Sacramento and still had every intention of marrying her. During the summer Beverly found out that there was a vacancy for a children's librarian in Yakima, Washington. She went to an interview and was offered a job. She would be paid $110 a month. For Beverly, this was a great deal of money.

Beverly moved to Yakima, lived in a boardinghouse, and began her work. The young people she met as a librarian were from all kinds of backgrounds, and she learned a lot from them. Years later she recalled, "Most vividly of all I remember the group of grubby little boys, nonreaders, who came once a week during school hours, marching in columns of two from nearby St. Joseph's School."[3]

Beverly found it challenging to locate books that they would like. One book fit the bill: *Honk the Moose,* by Phil Stong. This funny story is about a starving moose that wanders into a Minnesota town, and the two boys who feed it hay from their father's barn. It was one of the few children's books that appealed to boys. The search, she said, reminded her of "my own childhood reading, when I longed for funny stories about the sort of children who lived in my neighborhood."[4] These were the kinds of books that Beverly would one day write.

Clarence visited her during Christmas. He gave her an engagement ring and a promise to marry the following December. As it turned out, they decided to wed sooner. Since Mr. and Mrs. Bunn were still opposed to the marriage, Beverly and Clarence drove to Reno and got married without her parents' blessings in the fall of 1940.

Beverly quit her job and began her married life with Clarence in Sacramento. Though she had ended her career as a children's librarian, she would always hold the profession in high regard. She would later say, "Kids deserve books of literary quality, and librarians are so important in encouraging them to read."[5]

Beverly and Clarence moved a number of times in the early years of their marriage. They soon left Sacramento and moved to San Francisco and then to Oakland, which was closer to Clarence's work. Beverly got a job in Berkeley at the Sather Gate Bookshop, where she worked during the Christmas season. In December 1941, Beverly and Clarence were listening to the radio. They were stunned to find out that the Japanese had bombed Pearl Harbor, Hawaii. The United States had entered World War II, and Clarence worried about being drafted.

Because her bookstore job was only for the Christmas season, Beverly decided she needed another source of income. She found work at Camp John T. Knight, which was part of the Oakland Army Base. There she met a number of interesting men from all over the

United States. She enjoyed the people, but the job was stressful. She had a long commute and long hours. Finally, she found employment as a post librarian in an area station hospital being built at Hotel Oakland, which was closer to home. Beverly helped set up and organize the library. She worked there until the war ended.

Beverly and Clarence found a house to buy in Berkeley Hills, a place that Beverly had liked since her days at Cal. They ended up keeping the cat that had belonged to the previous owners, and "Kitty" became a valued member of the family. Years later Beverly would write a book about a cat called Socks, who was similar in many respects to Kitty. The Clearys lived near Quail, a woman who worked at the Sather Gate Bookshop. Quail lived with her mother, Hannah, an independent woman who became Beverly's good friend.

So far school, work, the war, and other activities had kept Beverly busy. Many years before, she had decided she was going to be a writer. When was it going to happen? Would it ever happen?

FYInfo

Women's Work During World War II

Rosie the Riveter

Before World War II (1939–1945), most middle-class married women were expected to stay home and tend to the house and children. Women who worked usually held traditional "feminine" jobs such teacher, librarian, or nurse. As soon as they married, if they could afford to stay home, most women quit their job to focus on running a household and raising a family.

When the United States entered World War II in 1941, companies—including those that produced airplanes and other military equipment—lost a great deal of their workforce. The men became soldiers and were sent overseas to fight. The U.S. government began a massive campaign to coax women into the workplace.

One way the government encouraged women was by using posters depicting women at work and reminding them that they were needed in the war effort. The most famous image was of Rosie the Riveter, a striking woman wearing blue coveralls. She looks at the viewer with a determined stare and is rolling back one sleeve to expose her well-developed biceps. The image of Rosie was supposed to show that women could be tough and beautiful in the war effort. But women were also attracted to the independence and money that work would provide.

At first, seeing women in nontraditional workplaces such as factories brought out some hostility from men. As time went on and women proved themselves, the men became more accepting.

After the war, women were encouraged to quit their jobs and return to their traditional roles as housekeepers and mothers. Not all of them were happy to leave their jobs. The joy of learning new skills and earning a higher wage than traditional women's work were hard to give up. Much later in the twentieth century, they would find their way back into the workforce, and some would seek the nontraditional jobs that women had held during World War II.

In 2003, Cleary (in red) won the National Medal of Arts Lifetime Honor Award. President George W. Bush (center) presented the award to (from left) Buddy Guy, a blues musician; Suzanne Farrell, a dancer and artistic director; Cleary; and actor-director Ron Howard.

Chapter 5

HENRY HUGGINS

All the years of college and work had kept Beverly Cleary's dream of writing a children's book alive, but lack of time and ideas for a book had kept it from coming true. Was writing *just* a dream? Finally, after another Christmas season at the Sather Gate Bookshop, Cleary decided to give it a go.

"On January 2, 1949, I gathered up my typewriter, freshly sharpened pencils, and the pile of paper and sat down. . . . *Write* and no backing out, I told myself,"[1] she remembered.

Cleary sat for a long time wondering what to write about. She knew that children liked stories, and she remembered the boys in Yakima who had had a hard time finding books they would enjoy. She thought of her own childhood in Portland. Then she imagined doing storytime again, telling a story boys would like: "Henry Huggins was in the third grade."[2] This was the first sentence in the story. Then she remembered an incident she had heard about children who tried to take their dog home in a streetcar. She used this idea for her story. "I soon discovered the pleasure of rearranging reality to suit myself. Two children became one, the streetcar became a bus, and so on."[3]

Cleary mailed out the story, and it was sent back to her with suggestions to make it work better as a book. Since it was a short story, the editor thought it would be hard to market. She suggested that Cleary bring together more of these little stories, add a plot, and create a book. Cleary set to work adding to the story of Henry and his dog, Spareribs. She added a number of chapters based on some of her own experiences growing up in Portland—including reworking the story she wrote in high school called "The Green Christmas." She also included other characters such as Beezus and her little sister Ramona.

All of the great writing advice she had heard over the years came back to her, including her mother's advice to "keep it simple" and "make it funny." Cleary finally finished the manuscript and sent it off to editor Elisabeth Hamilton of Morrow Junior Books.

Cleary waited anxiously for six weeks to get a response. Hamilton responded positively and noted that if Cleary were willing to make some revisions, they would like to publish the book. One of the revisions would be to change the name of the dog from Spareribs to Ribs or Ribsy. Cleary completed the revisions, and her book *Henry Huggins* was published in 1950.

Everyone in Beverly's family was proud of her. As she walked to the bank to deposit her check for her book, she thought about how she would continue to write. She remembered, "As I walked, I thought about all the bits of knowledge about children, reading, and writing that had clung to me like burrs or dandelion fluff all through childhood, college, the Yakima children's room and the bookstore."[4]

Cleary's writing career had just begun. More books about Henry came, as did stories of Ellen Tebbits, the girl who wanted to hide her woolen underwear when she attended ballet class.

Her most popular character first appeared as the little sister of Beezus (Beatrice) in *Henry Huggins*. Ramona Quimby, the pesky little sister, became the main character in *Ramona the Pest*, which was published in 1968. A number of Ramona books have been published since then, including *Ramona's World* in 1999. Cleary notes that Ramona didn't start out to be the star of her own series of books. She said, "[S]he was an accidental character. It occurred to me that as I wrote, all of these children appeared to be only children, so I tossed in a little sister."[5] This little sister, Ramona, went on to become a very well known and popular character. Cleary recalled, "Ramona comes out of my own childhood emotions, and I think all children pretty much have the same feelings."[6]

Cleary also wrote books for older readers. Junior high readers asked for books about teenagers. Drawing on some of her own experiences as a teen, she wrote *Jean and Johnny, Fifteen, Luckiest Girl,* and *Sister of the Bride.* Though most of her books are for grade-school readers, she has also written picture books for younger readers. *Two Times the Fun,* published in 2005, is a picture book about twins Jimmy and Janet.

An inspiration for Cleary's picture books came with the joy of having and raising twins of her own. In 1955, Marrienne Elizabeth and Malcolm James joined the Cleary family. Malcolm turned out to be a reluctant reader and decided he only wanted to read books about motorcycles. After watching Malcolm play with a toy motorcycle, Cleary wrote *The Mouse and the Motorcycle.* She explained that Malcolm "read and pronounced it a good book, sweet words to the mother of a non-reader."[7] Two more books about Ralph the Mouse and his motorcycle followed.

Departing from her usual lighthearted style, Beverly Cleary's *Dear Mr. Henshaw* (published in 1983) tells the story of a boy named Leigh Botts who writes letters to his favorite author, Mr. Henshaw. Leigh's letters reveal his frustrations and fears surrounding his parents' divorce. This book earned Cleary the prestigious Newbery Medal. The sequel was *Strider*, published in 1991. These books came about because readers asked Cleary to write a story about a child dealing with divorce.

Cleary's stories have been adapted for television as well. *Ramona* became a series on PBS in 1988, and the Ralph the Mouse books were made into three one-hour shows for ABC television.

Cleary has won a number of other awards over the years, including the Laura Ingalls Wilder Award, which honors authors who have made lasting contributions to children's literature. At the time, it was given only once every five years. Cleary was the fourth recipient after Wilder herself. In 2003, Cleary won the National Medal of Arts, the Lifetime Honor Award, which was presented by U.S. President George W. Bush. It was a fitting tribute to a very gifted writer who understands what it is like to be a child and have nothing good to read.

Another book award is actually named after Cleary. The Beverly Cleary Children's Choice Award is unique because it allows children to vote to decide their favorite books. Seven nominations are selected every year, and children can choose their favorite books from the alternatives. The award focuses on books for second- and third-graders, often books like Beverly's that have appealing characters to whom readers can relate.

On October 13, 1995, the Beverly Cleary Sculpture Garden was dedicated in Portland, Oregon. Beverly and Clarence stood next to life-sized sculptures of Henry, Ribsy, and Ramona in Grant Park near Grant High School, the same school Beverly had attended in the 1930s.

Cleary was also honored with the Beverly Cleary Endowed Professorship in Children's and Youth Services, which provides training and continuing education for librarians. This was created at the University of Washington, where Cleary had learned to be a librarian.

Though she grew up to become an award-winning author, Cleary hasn't forgotten the joys and fears of being a child. "In my books, I write for the child within myself,"[8] she said. Her books speak to the child in us all.

FYInfo

The John Newbery Medal

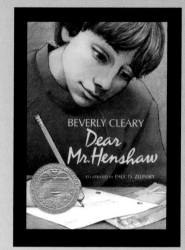

There are many prestigious awards given to book writers, but the first award designed for children's book authors was the John Newbery Medal. In 1922 the American Library Association began awarding the medal for the most distinguished American children's book published the previous year. They named the medal after an eighteenth-century English bookseller named John Newbery, who specialized in selling children's books. A committee reviews books that were written the previous year to select the prizewinner. They also select Newbery Honor books, which are runners-up to the Newbery Medal. These books receive awards for merit.

Over the years many popular books have won the Newbery. Prizewinning authors include Beverly Cleary, Lois Lowry, E. L. Konigsburg, Richard Peck, Linda Sue Park, and Cynthia Kadohata. Some of the books have been simply good stories with well-developed characters. Other award-winning books examine historical events or social issues as well. In Louis Sachar's award-winning book, *Holes,* young Stanley Yelnats has to go to a juvenile detention facility for a crime he didn't commit. At Camp Green Lake, he must dig a hole every day and soon learns that there is a reason behind the holes. The book *A Year Down Yonder,* by Richard Peck, is about fifteen-year-old Mary Alice and her adventures with her eccentric grandmother during the Depression era. *A Single Shard,* by Linda Sue Park, takes place in twelfth-century Korea. The book Cleary recommended to boys in Yakima in 1939, *Honk the Moose* by Phil Stong, was a Newbery Honor Book in 1936.

When an author is awarded a Newbery Medal, a golden seal with the medal design is placed on copies of the book. (The seal is silver on honor books.) The seal insures that readers know the special recognition the book has received.

CHRONOLOGY

1916 Born Beverly Atlee Bunn on April 12 in McMinnville, Oregon

1922 The Bunn family moves to Portland, Oregon

1930 Beverly begins attending Grant High School

1934 Graduates from Grant High School and goes to Ontario, California

1936 Graduates from Chaffey Junior College and begins her studies at "Cal" Berkeley

1938 Graduates from Cal and attends the University of Washington School of Librarianship

1939 Graduates from library school; begins working as a children's librarian in Yakima, Washington

1940 Marries Clarence Cleary; they live in California

1949 Begins writing *Henry Huggins*

1950 *Henry Huggins* is published

1955 Gives birth to twins, Malcolm James and Marrienne Elizabeth

1968 The first Ramona book, *Ramona the Pest,* is published

1975 The American Library Association presents her with the Laura Ingalls Wilder Award

1984 Wins the Newbery Medal for *Dear Mr. Henshaw*

1995 The Beverly Cleary Sculpture Garden is dedicated in Portland, Oregon

2003 Is awarded the National Medal of Arts, Lifetime Honor Award

2005 The Beverly Cleary Endowed Professorship in Children's and Youth Services is created at the University of Washington

2006 Work begins on a film based on Ramona Quimby, set for release in 2007

SELECTED WORKS

1950 *Henry Huggins*

1952 *Henry and Beezus*

1954 *Henry and Ribsy*

1956 *Fifteen*

1958 *The Luckiest Girl*

1959 *Jean and Johnny*

1963 *Sister of the Bride*

1965 *The Mouse and the Motorcycle*

1968 *Ramona the Pest*

1970 *Runaway Ralph*

1973 *Socks*

1975 *Ramona the Brave*

1977 *Ramona and Her Father*

1979 *Ramona and Her Mother*

1981 *Ramona Quimby, Age Eight*

1982 *Ralph S. Mouse*

1983 *Dear Mr. Henshaw*

1984 *Ramona Forever*

1988 *A Girl From Yamhill: A Memoir*

1991 *Strider*

1995 *My Own Two Feet: A Memoir*

1999 *Ramona's World*

2005 *Two Times the Fun*

TIMELINE IN HISTORY

1859	Oregon becomes the 33rd state in the United States.
1865	President Abraham Lincoln is shot.
1872	Lewis Carroll (mathematician Charles Dodgson) writes *Through the Looking Glass.*
1885	Carl Benz invents an automobile powered by an internal-combustion engine.
1903	Edwin Binney and C. Harold Smith invent crayons.
1914–1918	World War I is waged
1922	The first Newbery Medal is awarded to Hendrik Willem van Loon for *The Story of Mankind.*
1928	Walter E. Diemer invents bubble gum.
1931–1939	The Dust Bowl plagues the Midwestern and Southern plains of the United States.
1935	The Works Progress Administration is created, and the Social Security Act is signed into law.
1939–1945	World War II is waged.
1950	The first *Peanuts* cartoon strip, by Charles Schulz, is published.
1954	Laura Ingalls Wilder is given the first award in her name.
1963	The Reverend Martin Luther King Jr. delivers his "I have a dream" speech.
1977	The movie *Star Wars* is released.
2001	Terrorists attack the World Trade Center in New York City and the Pentagon in Washington, D.C.; U.S. President George W. Bush declares a "War on Terror."
2005	Hurricanes Katrina and Rita cause massive flooding in the city of New Orleans.
2006	The Bush administration's approval of the sale of major operations in six U.S. ports from a British-based company to Dubai's DP World, owned by the United Arab Emirates, sparks controversy across the United States.

CHAPTER NOTES

Chapter One　　　　**Blackbirds and Bluebirds**

1. Beverly Cleary, *A Girl From Yamhill: A Memoir* (New York: William Morrow, 1988), p. 77.

2. Ibid., p. 80.

3. Ibid., p. 83.

Chapter Two　　　　**Country Girl, City Girl**

1. Beverly Cleary, *A Girl From Yamhill: A Memoir* (New York: William Morrow, 1988), p. 11.

2. Ibid., p. 23.

3. Jennifer Marino, "A Conversation with Beverly Cleary," *Time For Kids,* April 8, 2005, http://www.timeforkids.com/TFK/news/story/0,6260,1046980,00.html

4. "Library Lifestyles of the Rich and Famous," an interview with Beverly Cleary, *American Libraries*, May 1996.

5. Cleary, p. 93.

6. Miriam Drennan, "I Can See Cleary Now," an interview with Beverly Cleary, *Book Page,* http://www.bookpage.com/9908bp/beverly_cleary.html

7. Cleary, p. 105.

8. Ibid., 109.

9. Ibid., p. 125.

10. Ibid., p. 145.

11. Ibid., p. 146.

12. Ibid., p. 147.

13. Ibid., p. 169.

Chapter Three　　　　**Writing and Boys**

1. Beverly Cleary, *A Girl From Yamhill: A Memoir* (New York: William Morrow, 1988), p. 228.

2. Ibid., p. 233.

3. Ibid., p. 241.

4. Ibid., p. 271.

5. Ibid., p. 272.

Chapter Four   Escape to California

1. Beverly Cleary, *My Own Two Feet: A Memoir* (New York: William Morrow, 1995), p. 9.

2. Ibid., p. 103.

3. Ibid., p. 236.

4. Ibid.

5. "Cleary Honored," *School Library Journal,* April 1, 2005, http://www.schoollibraryjournal.com/article/CA514031.html

Chapter Five   Henry Huggins

1. Beverly Cleary, *My Own Two Feet: A Memoir* (New York: William Morrow, 1995), p. 329.

2. Ibid.

3. Beverly Cleary, Introduction to *Henry Huggins* (New York: HarperCollins, 2000).

4. Cleary, *My Own Two Feet,* p. 345.

5. Miriam Drennan, "I Can See Cleary Now," an interview with Beverly Cleary, *Book Page,* http://www.bookpage.com/9908bp/beverly_cleary.html

6. Jennifer Marino, "A Conversation with Beverly Cleary," *Time For Kids,* April 8, 2005, http://www.timeforkids.com/TFK/news/story/0,6260,1046980,00.html

7. EPA's Top 100 Authors: "Cleary, Beverly." Educational Paperback Association, 2000, http://www.edupaperback.org/showauth.cfm?authid=21, written for *Eighth Book of Junior Authors and Illustrators,* New York: H.W. Wilson Company, 2000.

8. Lee Bennett Hopkins, "Times of Their Lives: Nine Authors and Illustrators Look Back on Significant Chapters from Their Illustrious Careers," *Publishers Weekly,* February 20, 1995.

FURTHER READING

For Young Adults

Cleary, Beverly. *A Girl From Yamhill: A Memoir.* New York: Morrow, 1988.
Cleary, Beverly. *Fifteen.* New York: HarperTrophy, 1996.
Cleary, Beverly. *Jean and Johnny.* New York: HarperTrophy, 1996.
Cleary, Beverly. *The Luckiest Girl.* New York: HarperTrophy, 1996.
Cleary, Beverly. *My Own Two Feet: A Memoir.* New York: Morrow, 1995.

Works Consulted

American Library Association. *Newbery Medal.* http://www.ala.org/ala/alsc/
    awardsscholarships/literaryawds/newberymedal/newberymedal.htm
Cleary, Beverly. *A Girl From Yamhill: A Memoir.* New York: Morrow, 1988.
———. *My Own Two Feet: A Memoir.* New York: Morrow, 1995.
"Cleary Honored." *School Library Journal.* April 1, 2005. http://
    www.schoollibraryjournal.com/article/CA514031.html
Drennan, Miriam. "I Can See Cleary Now." An interview with Beverly
    Cleary. *Book Page.* http://www.bookpage.com/9908bp/
    beverly_cleary.html
EPA's Top 100 Authors: "Cleary, Beverly." Educational Paperback
    Association, 2000. http://www.edupaperback.org/
    showauth.cfm?authid=21, written for *Eighth Book of Junior Authors and
    Illustrators,* New York: H.W. Wilson Company, 2000.
Hopkins, Lee Bennett. "Times of Their Lives: Nine Authors and Illustrators
    Look Back on Significant Chapters from Their Illustrious Careers"
    (excerpted from "Pauses: Autobiographical Reflections of 101
    Creators of Children's Books," by Lee Bennett Hopkins), *Publishers
    Weekly,* February 20, 1995, v242 n8 p131(2).
"The Laura Ingalls Wilder Award." American Library Association. http://
    www.ala.org/ala/alsc/awardsscholarships/literaryawds/wildermedal/
    wildermedal.htm
Maeterlinck, Maurice. *The Blue Bird: A Fairy Play in Six Acts.* Amsterdam, The
    Netherlands: Fredonia Books, 2001.
Marino, Jennifer. "A Conversation with Beverly Cleary." *Time For Kids.* http://
    www.timeforkids.com/TFK/news/story/0,6260,1046980,00.html
Nichols, Nancy A. "What Ever Happened to Rosie the Riveter?" *Harvard
    Business Review.* July/August. 1993.
Trinklein, Mike, and Steve Boettcher. "The Oregon Trail." Idaho State
    University, 2003. http://www.isu.edu/%7Etrinmich/Oregontrail.html

"Visit Ramona at Portland's Beverly Cleary Sculpture Garden for Children"
Multnomah County [Oregon] Library. http://www.multcolib.org/kids/
cleary/index.html

Watkins, T. H. *The Great Depression: America in the 1930s.* Boston: Little,
Brown and Company, 1993.

On the Internet

The Oregon Trail.
http://www.isu.edu/%7Etrinmich/Oregontrail.html

We Made Do—Recalling the Great Depression.
http://www.mcsc.k12.in.us/mhs/social/madedo/

The World of Beverly Cleary.
http://www.beverlycleary.com

GLOSSARY

coax
(KOKES)
To influence or gently urge.

depression
(dih-PREH-shun)
A period of low economic activity
marked by high unemployment rates.

idyllic
(eye-DIL-ik)
Pleasing and attractive in natural
simplicity.

irrational
(ih-RAH-shun-ul)
Done without thinking or nonsensically.

Persephone
(per-SEH-fuh-nee)
From Greek mythology, the
daughter of Demeter and Zeus
who marries Hades, god of the
underworld.

platoon
(plah-TOON)
A group of people who share a
common activity or characteristic.

smudge pot
A container of oil burned beside a
tree; the wind blows the smoke at
the tree, protecting it from frost.

tonsillitis
(tahn-suh-LIE-tis)
A disease of the tonsils, which are
at the back of the throat.

INDEX